# FRANK LLOYD WRIGHT

## 30 ARCHITECTURAL DRAWINGS

THE FRANK LLOYD WRIGHT FOUNDATION

D1232330

A BOOK OF POSTCARDS
POMEGRANATE ARTBOOKS, SAN FRANCISCO

Pomegranate Artbooks
Box 808022
Petaluma, CA 94975

ISBN 0-87654-822-2
Pomegranate Catalog No. A592

Pomegranate publishes two other architectural books of postcards, *Architecture 1900* and *The Art of Architecture*, as well as several others on many other subjects, including art, photography, music, historical figures and Hollywood. Please write to the publisher for more information.

© 1991 The Frank Lloyd Wright Foundation
Cover design by Zoe Katherine Burke

THE GREAT BEAUTY OF THESE DRAWINGS is evident in an unprecedented variety of forms. The work shown attests to the birth of a genuinely creative architecture at a time when all around the world architecture was moribund. For more than 500 years forms had been untrue to either time or man, and more recently the art of architecture was considered to be a matter of eclectic time-worn styles hung upon the framework of modern building techniques.

Steel, concrete, reinforced concrete, glass, new metals, plastics: these were the "miracles," as Frank Lloyd Wright termed them, of the twentieth century. These were the materials combined with the new methods of construction by which he freed architecture of its archaic bondage. He perceived new textures, shapes, spaces, thus made possible. The cantilever and steel reinforcing concrete abolished the ancient cliche of the box in architecture, and in its place came freedom and plasticity, continuity, flow of interior space and exterior form. Intrinsic unity, the sense of the whole as related to its parts, the parts in turn related to the whole, the quality of space embodied in form, became the innate character of the work he called *Organic Architecture*.

What he envisioned as countless new possibilities of architectural expression grew and expanded during his long creative life's work. The story of this revolution in architecture as originated by him is permanently recorded in the history of our era.

The reproductions of his original drawings provide a revelation of the poetry of the lifetime quest by Frank Lloyd Wright for the expression of beauty, and its inevitable fulfillment for the life of mankind.

—Bruce Brooks Pfeiffer, Director of Archives, The Frank Lloyd Wright Foundation

**FRANK LLOYD WRIGHT**
**"Fallingwater," House for Edgar J. Kaufmann**
Bear Run, Pennsylvania, 1935
Perspective, 33 x 17 in. Graphite pencil and color
pencil on white tracing paper

Pomegranate • Box 808022 • Petaluma, CA 94975

© The Frank Lloyd Wright Foundation

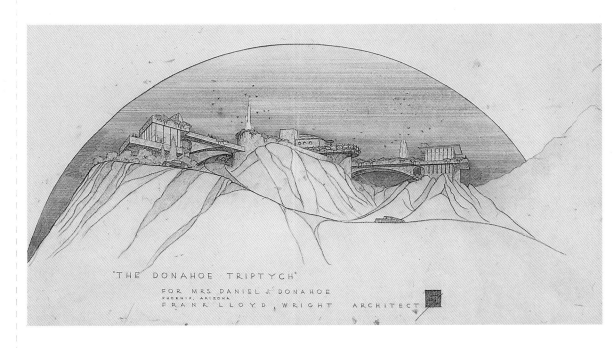

"THE DONAHOE TRIPTYCH"

FOR MRS. DANIEL J. DONAHOE
PHOENIX, ARIZONA
FRANK LLOYD WRIGHT ARCHITECT

**FRANK LLOYD WRIGHT**
**Project: "Donahoe Triptych," House for Helen**
**Donahoe**
Paradise Valley, Arizona, 1959
Perspective, 58 x 55 in. Graphite pencil and color
pencil on white tracing paper

Pomegranate • Box 808022 • Petaluma, CA 94975

© The Frank Lloyd Wright Foundation

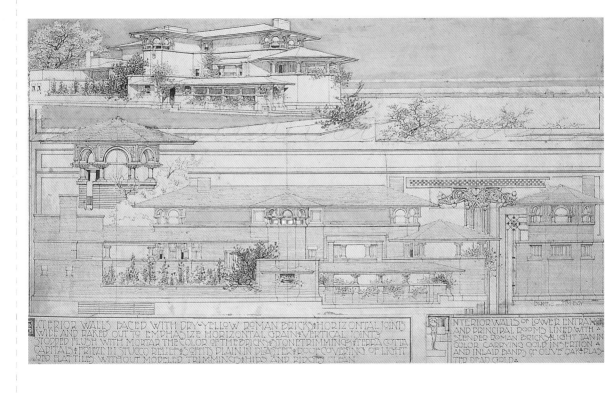

EXTERIOR WALLS FACED WITH DRY YELLOW ROMAN BRICKS HORIZONTAL JOINTS
WIDE AND RAKED OUT TO EMPHASIZE HORIZONTAL GRAIN VERTICAL JOINTS
STOPPED FLUSH WITH MORTAR THE COLOR OF THE BRICKS STONE TRIMMINGS TERRA COTTA
CAPITALS FRIEZE IN STUCCO RELIEF SOFFIT PLAIN IN PLASTER ROOF COVERING OF LIGHT
RED FLAT TILES WITHOUT MODELED TRIMMINGS HIPS AND RIDGES CLEAN

INTERIOR WALLS OF LOWER ENTRANCE
AND PRINCIPAL ROOMS LINED WITH A
SLENDER ROMAN BRICKS LIGHT TAN IN
COLOR CARRYING GOLD INSERTION
AND INLAID BANDS OF OLIVE OAK PLAS-
TER DEAD GOLD

**FRANK LLOYD WRIGHT**
**House for Joseph Husser**
Chicago, Illinois, 1899
Publication-exhibition drawing containing view,
elevation and details, 21 x 12 in. Sepia ink and
watercolor wash on off-white paper

Pomegranate • Box 808022 • Petaluma, CA 94975

© The Frank Lloyd Wright Foundation

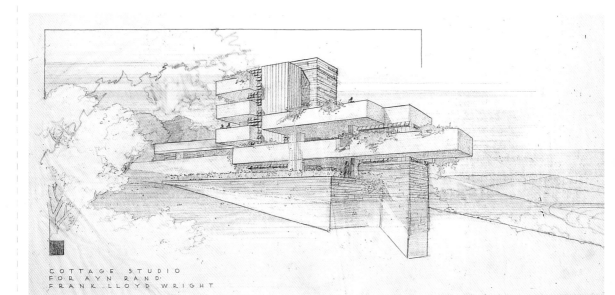

COTTAGE STUDIO
FOR AYN RAND
FRANK LLOYD WRIGHT

**FRANK LLOYD WRIGHT**
**Project: House and Studio for Ayn Rand**
Hollywood, California, 1946
Perspective, 37 x 25 in. Graphite pencil and color
pencil on white tracing paper

Pomegranate • Box 808022 • Petaluma, CA 94975

© The Frank Lloyd Wright Foundation

**FRANK LLOYD WRIGHT**
**Solomon R. Guggenheim Museum**
New York, New York, 1943–59
Perspective: night rendering, 40 x 25½ in. Watercolor
and tempera on black illustration board

Pomegranate • Box 808022 • Petaluma, CA 94975

© The Frank Lloyd Wright Foundation

**FRANK LLOYD WRIGHT**
**A. D. German Warehouse**
Richland Center, Wisconsin, 1915
Perspective, 24⅜ x 21½ in. India ink, graphite pencil,
watercolor and color pencil on tracing cloth (linen)

Pomegranate • Box 808022 • Petaluma, CA 94975

© The Frank Lloyd Wright Foundation

**FRANK LLOYD WRIGHT**
**House for K. C. DeRhodes**
South Bend, Indiana, 1906
Perspective, 26 x 19 in. Sepia ink and watercolor
wash on off-white art paper

Pomegranate • Box 808022 • Petaluma, CA 94975

© The Frank Lloyd Wright Foundation

**FRANK LLOYD WRIGHT**
**Francis Apartments**
Chicago, Illinois, 1895
Perspective, 24 x 14 in. India ink on white tracing
paper

Pomegranate • Box 808022 • Petaluma, CA 94975

© The Frank Lloyd Wright Foundation

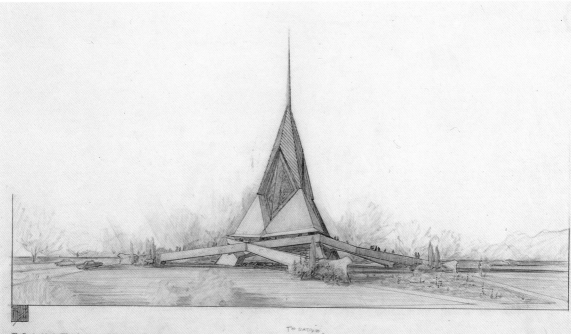

TRINITY CHAPEL
NORMAN , OKLAHOMA

FRANK LLOYD WRIGHT , ARCHITECT

**FRANK LLOYD WRIGHT**
**Project: Trinity Chapel, University of Oklahoma**
Norman, Oklahoma, 1958
Perspective, 49 x 35⅝ in. Graphite pencil and color
pencil on white tracing paper

Pomegranate • Box 808022 • Petaluma, CA 94975

© The Frank Lloyd Wright Foundation

**FRANK LLOYD WRIGHT**
**Project: Point View Residences**
Pittsburgh, Pennsylvania, 1952
Perspective, 31 x 37 in. Pencil and color pencil on
tracing paper

Pomegranate • Box 808022 • Petaluma, CA 94975

© The Frank Lloyd Wright Foundation

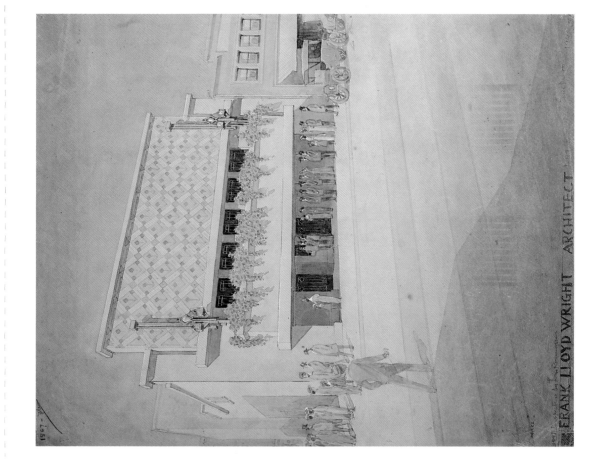

FRANK LLOYD WRIGHT ARCHITECT

**FRANK LLOYD WRIGHT**
**Project: Cinema San Diego**
San Diego, California, 1915
Perspective, 15 x 19 in. Watercolor and watercolor
wash on art paper

Pomegranate • Box 808022 • Petaluma, CA 94975

© The Frank Lloyd Wright Foundation

**FRANK LLOYD WRIGHT**
**Project: "Seacliff," V. C. Morris House**
San Francisco, California, 1945
Perspective, 42 x 40 in. Pencil and color pencil on
tracing paper

Pomegranate • Box 808022 • Petaluma, CA 94975

© The Frank Lloyd Wright Foundation

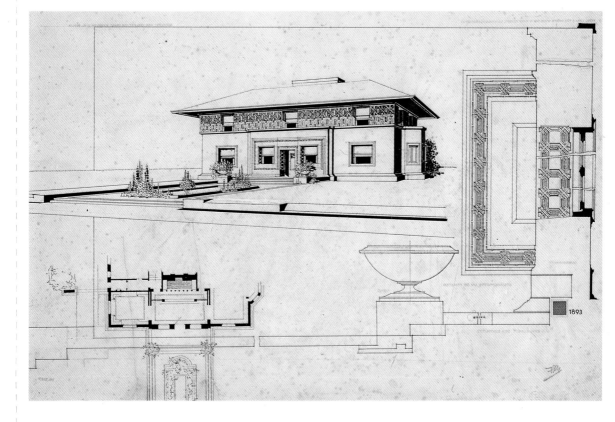

1893

**FRANK LLOYD WRIGHT**
**House for William H. Winslow**
River Forest, Illinois, 1893
Plan, perspective and ornamental details, 23 x 16 in.
India ink on white tracing paper

Pomegranate • Box 808022 • Petaluma, CA 94975

© The Frank Lloyd Wright Foundation

**FRANK LLOYD WRIGHT**
**Project: A. K. McAfee House**
Kenilworth, Illinois, 1894
Perspective, 29 x 10 in. Watercolor and watercolor
wash on art paper

Pomegranate • Box 808022 • Petaluma, CA 94975

© The Frank Lloyd Wright Foundation

**FRANK LLOYD WRIGHT**
**Project: House for Raul Bailleres**
Acapulco, Mexico, 1952
Perspective, 53 x 32 in. Graphite pencil and color
pencil, blue ink and sepia ink on white tracing paper
mounted to board

Pomegranate • Box 808022 • Petaluma, CA 94975

© The Frank Lloyd Wright Foundation

**FRANK LLOYD WRIGHT**
**Project: Civic Center for Pittsburgh Point**
Pittsburgh, Pennsylvania, 1947
Perspective, 75 x 33 in. Graphite pencil, color pencil,
India and blue ink on white tracing paper, mounted to
board

Pomegranate • Box 808022 • Petaluma, CA 94975

© The Frank Lloyd Wright Foundation

PRO BONO PUBLICO ARIZONA
"OASIS"
FRANK LLOYD WRIGHT ARCHITECT

**FRANK LLOYD WRIGHT**
**Project: "Oasis," Arizona State Capitol**
Phoenix, Arizona, 1957
Night perspective, 40 x 32 in. Tempera, watercolor
and pastel on black illustration board

Pomegranate • Box 808022 • Petaluma, CA 94975

© The Frank Lloyd Wright Foundation

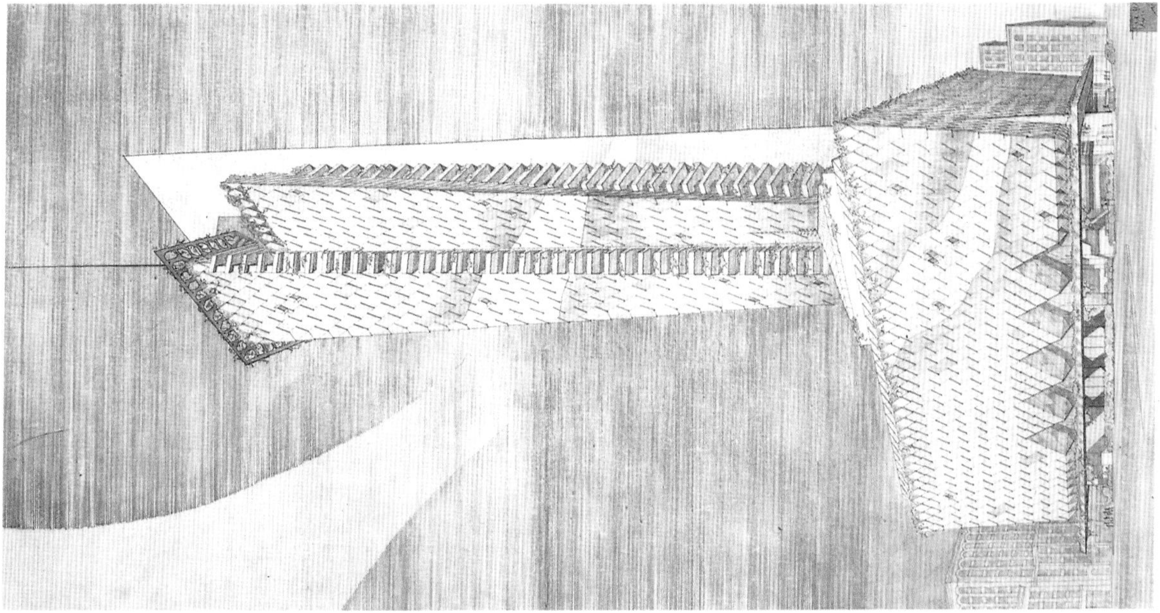

**FRANK LLOYD WRIGHT**
**Project: The Rogers Lacy Hotel for Rogers Lacy**
Dallas, Texas, 1946
Perspective, 24¼ x 53⅛ in. Graphite pencil, color
pencil and India ink on Japanese paper

Pomegranate • Box 808022 • Petaluma, CA 94975

© The Frank Lloyd Wright Foundation

**FRANK LLOYD WRIGHT**
**Ravine Bluffs Bridge**
Glencoe, Illinois, 1915
Perspective, 23½ x 17½ in. Watercolor on tan art
paper

Pomegranate • Box 808022 • Petaluma, CA 94975

© The Frank Lloyd Wright Foundation

MR. C. THAXTER SHAW
RESIDENCE · MONTRE
DINING ROOM
FRANK LLOYD WRIGHT
ARCHITECT
OAK PARK · ILLINOIS

**FRANK LLOYD WRIGHT**
**Remodelled House for C. Thaxter Shaw**
Montreal, Canada, 1906
Interior perspective of dining room, 15 x 7 in.
Watercolor and ink on off-white tracing paper

Pomegranate • Box 808022 • Petaluma, CA 94975

© The Frank Lloyd Wright Foundation

**FRANK LLOYD WRIGHT**
**Unity Temple**
Oak Park, Illinois, 1904
Perspective, 25⅛ x 12 in. Watercolor and sepia ink on
off-white art paper

Pomegranate • Box 808022 • Petaluma, CA 94975

© The Frank Lloyd Wright Foundation

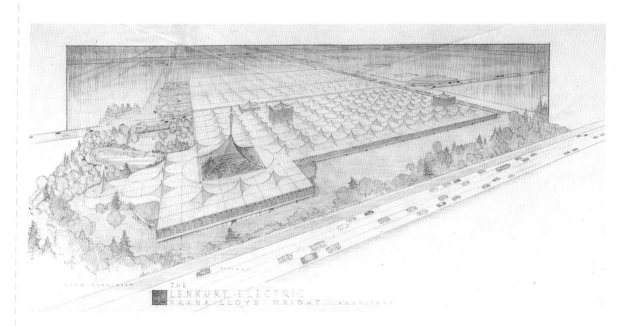

VIEW FROM REAR

THE LENKURT ELECTRIC
FRANK LLOYD WRIGHT ARCHITECT

**FRANK LLOYD WRIGHT**
**Project: Lenkurt Electric Company**
San Carlos, California, 1955
Aerial perspective, 64 x 37 in. Pencil and color pencil
on tracing paper

Pomegranate • Box 808022 • Petaluma, CA 94975

© The Frank Lloyd Wright Foundation

**FRANK LLOYD WRIGHT**
**Project: Gordon Strong Planetarium**
Sugar Loaf Mountain, Maryland, 1924
Perspective, 31 x 20 in. Color pencil and pencil on
tracing paper

Pomegranate • Box 808022 • Petaluma, CA 94975

© The Frank Lloyd Wright Foundation

**FRANK LLOYD WRIGHT**
**Project: "A Home in a Prairie Town" for** *Ladies'*
*Home Journal,* 1900
Perspective, 25 x 15 in. Watercolor and watercolor
wash on art paper

Pomegranate • Box 808022 • Petaluma, CA 94975

© The Frank Lloyd Wright Foundation

**FRANK LLOYD WRIGHT**
**Project: Lake Tahoe Summer Colony**
Lake Tahoe, California, 1922
Perspective, 15 x 22 in. Pencil and color pencil on
tracing paper

Pomegranate • Box 808022 • Petaluma, CA 94975

© The Frank Lloyd Wright Foundation

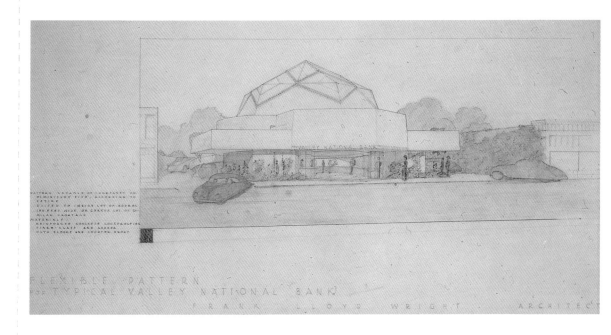

PATTERN CAPABLE OF INCREASED OR
DIMINISHED SIZE, ACCORDING TO
DESIRE
SUITED TO INSIDE LOT OR ADDED
100 FEET WIDE OR CORNER LOT OF 5-
MILES FRONTAGE
MATERIAL T
REINFORCED CONCRETE CONSTRUCTION
FIBRE GLASS AND COPPER
COYA BLOCKS AND COUNTER FRONT

FLEXIBLE  PATTERN
FOR TYPICAL VALLEY NATIONAL BANK

F R A N K    L L O Y D    W R I G H T    A R C H I T E C T

**FRANK LLOYD WRIGHT**
**Project: "Daylight Bank" for Valley National Bank**
Tucson, Arizona, 1947
Perspective, 39 x 26 in. Pencil and color pencil on
tracing paper

Pomegranate • Box 808022 • Petaluma, CA 94975

© The Frank Lloyd Wright Foundation

**FRANK LLOYD WRIGHT**
**Project: Twin Bridges for Point Park**
Pittsburgh, Pennsylvania, 1948
Perspective, 44 x 29 in.
Pencil and color pencil on tracing paper

Pomegranate • Box 808022 • Petaluma, CA 94975

© The Frank Lloyd Wright Foundation

**FRANK LLOYD WRIGHT**
**Project: E. L. Marting House**
Northampton, Ohio, 1947
Perspective, 43 x 22 in. Pencil and color pencil on
tracing paper

Pomegranate • Box 808022 • Petaluma, CA 94975

© The Frank Lloyd Wright Foundation

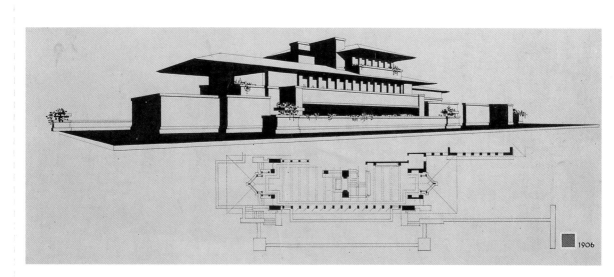

1906

**FRANK LLOYD WRIGHT**
**House for Frederick C. Robie**
Chicago, Illinois, 1907
Perspective and partial plan, 37½ x 21½ in. Sepia ink
on tan art paper

Pomegranate • Box 808022 • Petaluma, CA 94975

© The Frank Lloyd Wright Foundation

**FRANK LLOYD WRIGHT**
**House for Isidore Heller**
Chicago, Illinois, 1896
Perspective, 30 x 10½ in. Watercolor and graphite
pencil on tracing paper mounted to heavy grade art
paper

Pomegranate • Box 808022 • Petaluma, CA 94975

© The Frank Lloyd Wright Foundation